FRANCE
EXPLORE THE COUNTRIES
EXPLORE THE COUNTRIES
EXPLORE THE COUNTRIES
Big Buddy BOOKS
Explore the Countries
Sarah Tieck

**VISIT US AT**
**www.abdopublishing.com**

Published by ABDO Publishing Company, PO Box 398166, Minneapolis, MN 55439.



Printed in the United States of America, North Mankato, Minnesota.
042013
112013
PRINTED ON RECYCLED PAPER

Coordinating Series Editor: Rochelle Baltzer
Contributing Editors: Megan M. Gunderson, Marcia Zappa
Graphic Design: Adam Craven
Cover Photograph: *Shutterstock*: WDG Photo.
Interior Photographs/Illustrations: *AP Photo*: AP Photo (p. 15), Laurent Cipriani (p. 29), North Wind Picture Archives via AP Images (p. 31), Rex Features via AP Images (p. 25), Kenzo Tribouillard, Pool (p. 19); *Getty Images*: DeAgostini (pp. 13, 17), DEA/M. SEEMULLER (p. 33); *Glow Images*: SuperStock (p. 16); *iStockphoto*: ©iStockphoto.com/kodachrome25 (p. 25); *Shutterstock*: Leonid Andronov (p. 34), DGF72 (p. 23), Globe Turner (pp. 19, 38), Iakov Kalinin (p. 5), Zoran Karapancev (p. 9), LiliGraphie (p. 34), luri (p. 35), Maisna (p. 27), Christian Musat (p. 21), Maryna Pleshkun (p. 38), Patrick Poendl (p. 11), Samot (p. 9), Worakit Sirijinda (p. 35), spectrumblue (p. 27), Boris Stroujko (p. 11), syaochka (p. 37), TonyV3112 (p. 35), Keith Wheatley (p. 23).

Country population and area figures taken from the CIA World Factbook.

**Library of Congress Control Number: 2013932152**

**Cataloging-in-Publication Data**

Tieck, Sarah.
France / Sarah Tieck.
p. cm. -- (Explore the countries)
ISBN 978-1-61783-810-1 (lib. bdg.)
1. France--Juvenile literature. I. Title.
944--dc23

2013932152

# Contents

# Around the World

Our world has many countries. Each country has beautiful land. It has its own rich history. And, the people have their own languages and ways of life.

France is a country in Europe. What do you know about France? Let's learn more about this place and its story!

**Did You Know?**

French is the official language of France.

The Eiffel Tower is a famous monument in Paris. When it was finished in 1889, it was the world's tallest structure!

# Passport to France

France is a country in western Europe. Seven countries border it. It is also bordered by the Atlantic Ocean and the Mediterranean Sea. Corsica is a French island in the Mediterranean Sea.

France's total area is 248,573 square miles (643,801 sq km). About 66 million people live there.

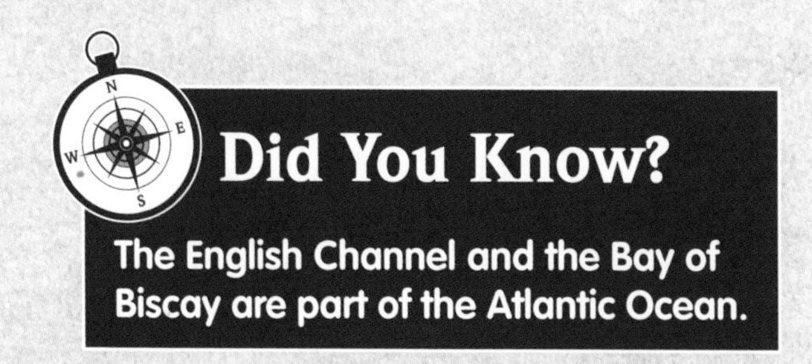

**Did You Know?**

The English Channel and the Bay of Biscay are part of the Atlantic Ocean.

# WHERE IN THE WORLD?

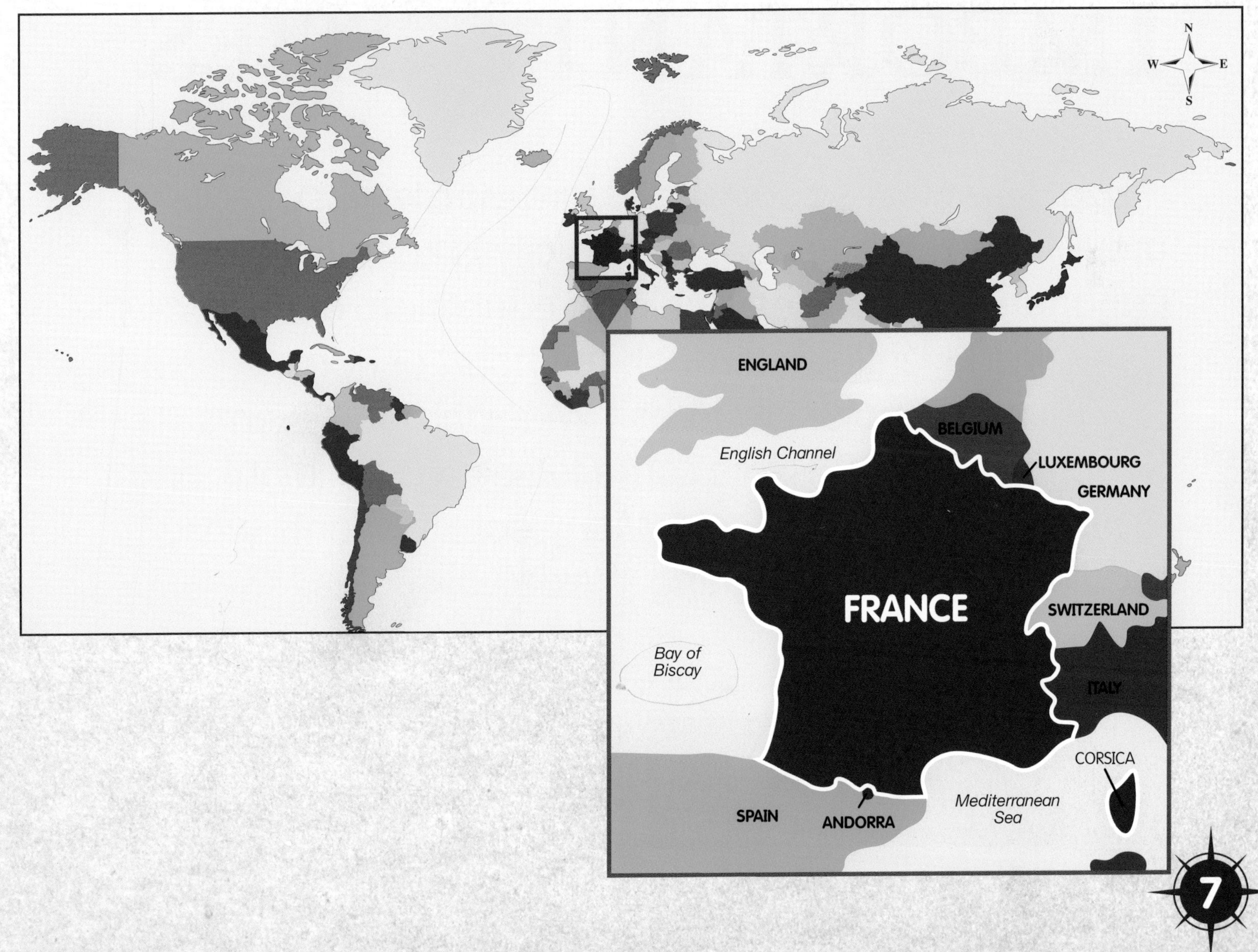

# IMPORTANT CITIES

Paris is France's **capital** and largest city, with more than 2 million people. This city is known for its importance to business, politics, education, and the arts. The Seine River flows through the heart of Paris.

Paris is a popular city to visit. Many historic events happened there. Visitors come to see old buildings and walk or bike on city streets. Many eat croissants while reading or people watching in sidewalk cafés.

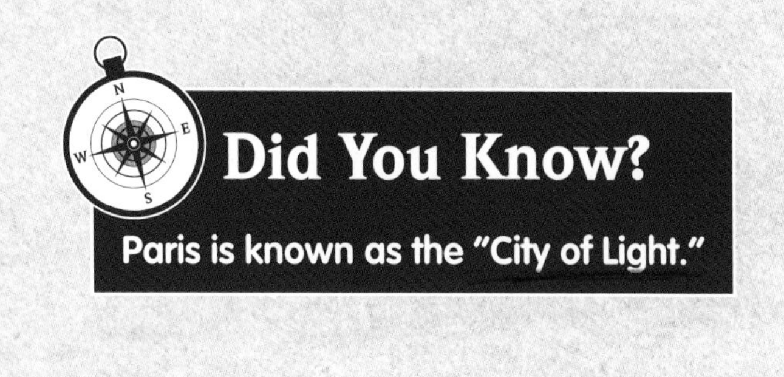


**Did You Know?**

Paris is known as the "City of Light."

**SAY IT**

**Paris**
*PA-ruhs*

**Seine**
*SAYN*

The Arc de Triomphe is a famous monument in Paris. Known for its size, it stands about 164 feet (50 m) high!

Notre-Dame is a historic church in Paris. Building started in 1163.

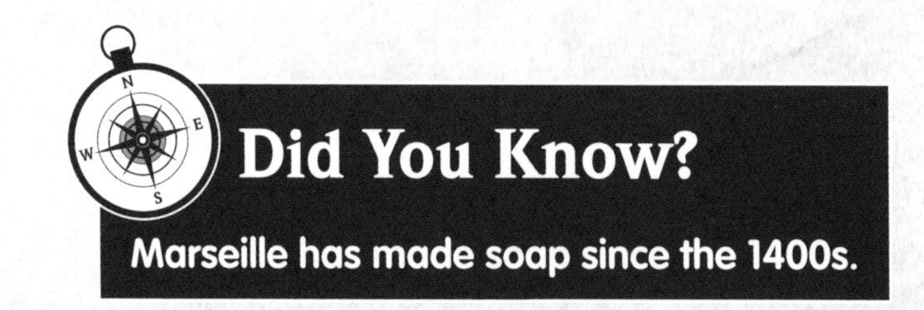


Marseille is France's second-largest city. It has about 840,000 people. Founded around 600 BC, it is the country's oldest large city and most important port. The port is on the Mediterranean Sea.

Lyon is France's third-largest city, with more than 470,000 people. The Rhône and Saône Rivers meet in this historic city. Cloth, such as silk and rayon, is made there. The area is also known for its wine and cheese. From Lyon, people travel to Paris and Marseille using fast trains called the TGV.

Visitors to Marseille shop and eat in the Old Port area.

Vieux Lyon, or Old Lyon, is known for having beautiful buildings from the Renaissance. This was a time period from the 1300s to the 1600s in Europe.

# France in History

In ancient times, France was known as Gaul. The people of Gaul were called **Celts**. Around 50 BC, Romans took over Gaul. They ruled the land for about 500 years. Then, Franks took over.

One powerful Frankish ruler was Charlemagne. After he died, his **empire** broke apart. The western part became what is now France.

Over time, French rulers gained power. Around 1700, French people had little control. Most paid high taxes to support the government and the army. In 1789, they began a fight to change this. This was called the French **Revolution**.

Louis XVI ruled France during the French Revolution. He was killed in 1793.

After the French **Revolution**, the people made France a **republic**. In 1799, Napoleon I took over the country and became its ruler. He won many wars. Then in 1814, kings began ruling France again. In 1870, the country once again became a republic.

Many battles took place in France during **World War I** and **World War II**. The wars used up much of the country's **resources**. And, many people died. After 1945, the French began to rebuild their country. Today, France is a strong country.

In 1940, German troops took over Paris. Parisians were freed in 1944.

# Timeline

**1429**

At about age 17, Joan of Arc led French soldiers. With her help, they won an important battle against English soldiers in the Hundred Years' War.

**1793**

The Louvre Museum opened as an art museum in Paris. Before this, it was used as a palace.

**About 1867**

A group of French artists began painting in a new style. Known as impressionism, this style shows the effects of light on objects. Claude Monet, Edgar Degas, and Paul Cézanne became famous for this style.

## 1889

People saw the Eiffel Tower for the first time at a world's fair. It was built to honor the French **Revolution**.

## 1919

The Treaty of Versailles was signed at the Palace of Versailles. It ended **World War I**.

## 2012

Presidential elections were held in April and May. In a close race, François Hollande beat then-president Nicolas Sarkozy.

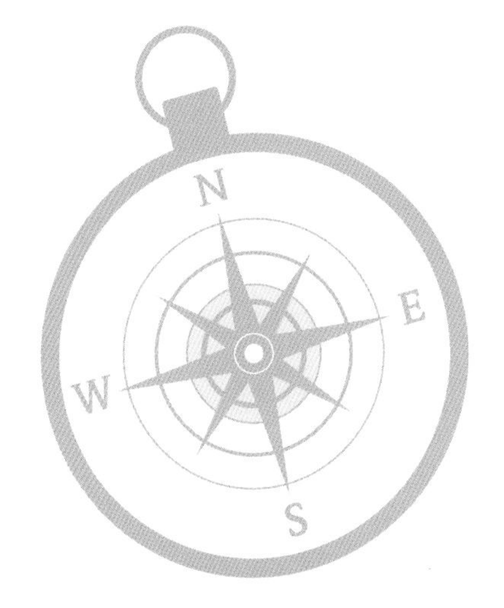

# An Important Symbol

France's flag was first used in 1794. It is called the French Tricolor. It has blue, white, and red. Blue and red stood for the city of Paris. White stood for the king.

France's government is a **republic**. There are 22 régions. France's parliament makes laws. The president is the head of state. The prime minister is the head of government.

Before 1848, France's flag changed often.

In 2012, François Hollande became France's president.

# Across the Land

France has mountains, coasts, cliffs, hills, and flat areas. Much of the land is covered with farms and fields.

The French Alps are in southeast France. They are home to Mont Blanc, the country's highest point. The Pyrenees Mountains are in the southwest. The cliffs of Normandy are in northern France.

The Loire is the longest river in France. The Rhine and Seine Rivers also flow through the country.

**Did You Know?**

In January, the average temperature in Paris is 28°F (-2°C). In July, it is 68°F (20°C).

The cliffs of Normandy are famous for their history. In 1944, an important World War II invasion happened there.

Many types of animals make their homes in France. These include Alpine marmots, hares, foxes, and chamois. Jellyfish and oysters live in the coastal waters.

France's land is home to a variety of plants. Lavender and wildflowers grow there. Chestnut, pine, and beech trees are also found in France.

Alpine marmots often live in mountain areas.

Poppies grow in the French countryside.

# EARNING A LIVING

France makes many products. The country's factories make cars, perfumes, medicines, cosmetics, glass, and tires. Others process foods such as cheese, wine, butter, and sugar. Many people have jobs in trade, health care, education, or banking. Others have jobs helping visitors.

France has important natural **resources**. Salt, stone, and gravel are mined there. Forests provide wood. Apples, grapes, sugar beets, and wheat grow in rich farm soil.

France has vineyards in areas such as Bordeaux and Champagne. Grapes are grown there.

France's fashion industry is world famous.

# Life in France

France is a modern country. It is known for its beauty and its history. Many famous artists, writers, and thinkers have come from this country. Today, people travel to France to experience its art, fashion, food, and land.

French foods include sauces, cheeses, breads, and pastries. Breakfast is a light meal. But, lunch and dinner often include soup, a main course, salad, and cheese or fruit. Meals often include wine, since France is famous for making it.

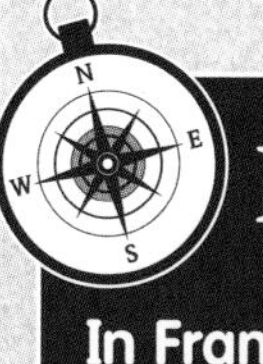


## Did You Know?

In France, children must attend school from ages 6 to 16. There are public nursery schools for children ages 2 to 6.

France is famous for its style of cooking. Some popular dishes include quiche (*right*) and crêpes.

Artists can be seen painting the streets of Paris or the lavender fields of Provence.

France is famous for a bicycle race called the Tour de France. The race takes place for about three weeks every July. The French also enjoy football, or soccer. Other common activities include fishing and swimming. Boules, or lawn bowling, is a popular game.

Religion is important in France. People mainly belong to the Roman Catholic Church. Many of France's holidays are connected with the church. One famous celebration is Carnival in Nice.

Tour de France racers bike more than 2,000 miles (3,200 km) throughout France and sometimes nearby countries. There are usually about 200 racers!

# FAMOUS FACES

Napoleon I was a famous military leader and **emperor**. He was born on August 15, 1769, in Corsica.

Napoleon joined the French army at age 16. He became a military hero. In 1799, he took control of France's government.

In 1804, Napoleon became emperor of France. He won many battles and helped France gain land. But, he also lost battles. He had to give up his title and leave France for good in 1815. Napoleon died in 1821.

Napoleon I was also called Napoléon Bonaparte. He was famous for being short. He was also known for having a temper!

Many talented people are from France. Victor Hugo was a famous writer. He was born on February 26, 1802, in Besançon. Hugo was known for leading the **Romantic** writing movement. He was also known for his interest in politics and history.

Hugo wrote poems, books, and essays. His famous book *The Hunchback of Notre Dame* was first printed in 1831. *Les Misérables* also became very famous. It came out in 1862. Hugo died in 1885.

Hugo's books are still popular. Some have been made into musicals and movies.

# Tour Book

Have you ever been to France? If you visit the country, here are some places to go and things to do!

## Explore

Visit Grand Île in Strasbourg. Some say it looks like a fairy-tale town. People go there to see the shops and bridges.

## Play

Spend time on the French Riviera. This is a popular resort area on the Mediterranean Sea. People vacation there and enjoy the beach.

## Discover

Explore Provence. This area is famous for its beauty, lavender fields, and style of cooking. Many artists have painted it. Famous American cook Julia Child visited Provence many times.

## Learn

Visit the Louvre Museum. It covers more than 40 acres (16 ha)! Take in world-famous paintings, such as Leonardo da Vinci's *Mona Lisa*.

## Remember

See the Palace of Versailles. It is known for its gardens and beauty. During the French Revolution, it was home to King Louis XVI and Queen Marie-Antoinette.

# A GREAT COUNTRY

The story of France is important to our world. The people and places that make up this country offer something special. They help make the world a more beautiful, interesting place.

Mont-Saint-Michel is a famous island off the coast of Normandy. An abbey was built atop a rock there starting in 966.

# France Up Close

**Official Name:** République Française (French Republic)

**Flag:**

**Population (rank):** 65,630,692 (July 2012 est.) (21st most-populated country)

**Total Area (rank):** 248,573 square miles (43rd largest country)

**Capital:** Paris

**Official Language:** French

**Currency:** Euro

**Form of Government:** Republic

**National Anthem:** "La Marseillaise"

# Important Words

**capital** a city where government leaders meet.

**Celts** (KEHLTS) people who lived about 2,000 years ago in many countries of western Europe.

**emperor** the male ruler of an empire.

**empire** a large group of states or countries under one ruler called an emperor or empress.

**republic** a government in which the people choose the leader.

**resource** a supply of something useful or valued.

**revolution** the forced overthrow of a government for a new system.

**Romantic** of or relating to Romanticism. This was a style of writing, art, and music based on feeling rather than reason. It was popular in the late 1700s and the 1800s.

**World War I** a war fought in Europe from 1914 to 1918.

**World War II** a war fought in Europe, Asia, and Africa from 1939 to 1945.

# Web Sites

To learn more about France, visit ABDO Publishing Company online. Web sites about France are featured on our Book Links page. These links are routinely monitored and updated to provide the most current information available.

**www.abdopublishing.com**

# Index